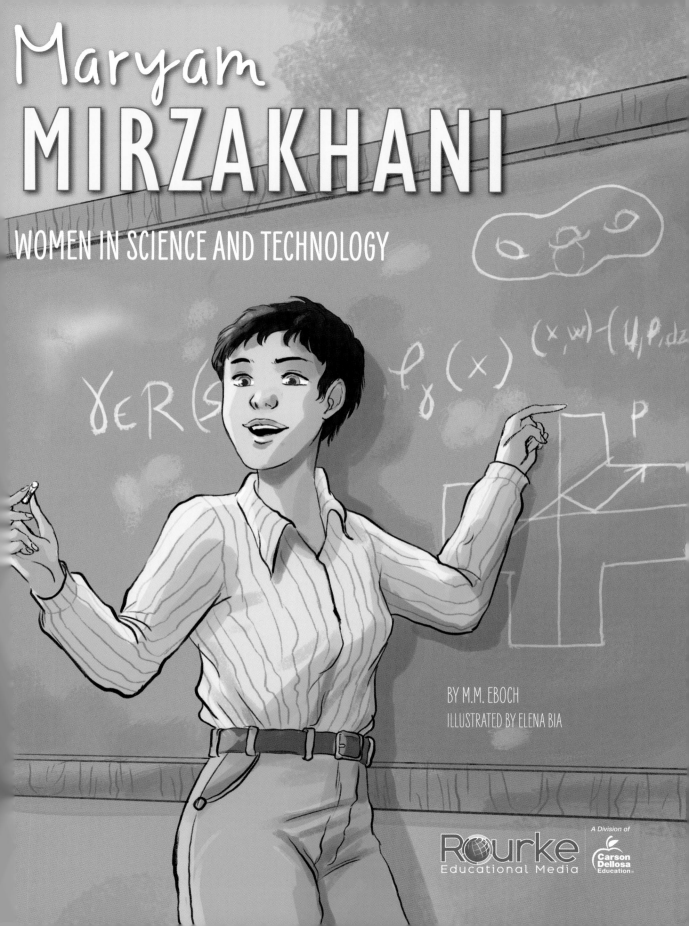

Before Reading: *Building Background Knowledge and Vocabulary*

Building background knowledge can help children process new information and build upon what they already know. Before reading a book, it is important to tap into what children already know about the topic. This will help them develop their vocabulary and increase their reading comprehension.

Questions and Activities to Build Background Knowledge:

1. Look at the front cover of the book and read the title. What do you think this book will be about?
2. What do you already know about this topic?
3. Take a book walk and skim the pages. Look at the table of contents, photographs, captions, and bold words. Did these text features give you any information or predictions about what you will read in this book?

Vocabulary: *Vocabulary Is Key to Reading Comprehension*

Use the following directions to prompt a conversation about each word.

- Read the vocabulary words.
- What comes to mind when you see each word?
- What do you think each word means?

Vocabulary Words:
- ambition
- competition
- diagrams
- disadvantage
- formulas
- international
- mathematics
- Persian

During Reading: *Reading for Meaning and Understanding*

To achieve deep comprehension of a book, children are encouraged to use close reading strategies. During reading, it is important to have children stop and make connections. These connections result in deeper analysis and understanding of a book.

 Close Reading a Text

During reading, have children stop and talk about the following:

- Any confusing parts
- Any unknown words
- Text to text, text to self, text to world connections
- The main idea in each chapter or heading

Encourage children to use context clues to determine the meaning of any unknown words. These strategies will help children learn to analyze the text more thoroughly as they read.

When you are finished reading this book, turn to the next-to-last page for **Text-Dependent Questions** and an **Extension Activity**.

TABLE OF CONTENTS

THE JOY OF MATH

Maryam Mirzakhani grew up in Tehrān, Iran. She liked to read and watch TV shows about inspirational women. These stories made her realize she could do something great with her life too! She had **ambition.**

"I thought I would become a writer one day," Maryam said.

Iran

Iran is a country in western Asia. Tehrān is the capital and largest city. The country was at war when Maryam was a young child.

But then Maryam learned more math. At first, she said, "I got excited about it maybe just as a challenge." She saw how fun math could be. Even though it could be fun, math wasn't always easy for Maryam. She had a teacher who told her she wasn't talented. This discouraged her, but she didn't let it stop her.

In middle school, she made a friend she would keep for life. Maryam and Roya Beheshti encouraged each other's love of math. Sometimes the two made math a **competition**. "Maryam's work was driven by a certain pure joy," Roya said.

BREAKING BARRIERS

The **International** Mathematical Olympiad is a math competition for high school students. Iran had never sent a girl to compete. Maryam and Roya wanted to go anyway. The high school for boys had more math classes than the girls' school. This put the girls at a **disadvantage** in the competition. They asked their principal for new classes.

Their principal listened to them. She believed Maryam and Roya could be the first girls to go to the International Mathematical Olympiad. They got the classes.

Maryam was able go to the International Mathematical Olympiad. She won a gold medal. The next year, she went back. She won another gold medal, and she got a perfect score!

Maryam studied math in college in Iran. "You have to spend some energy and effort to see the beauty of math," she said. "The more I spent time on **mathematics**, the more excited I became."

After Maryam graduated, she decided to go to graduate school in America. English was not her first language. She took her class notes in **Persian**. She did not always understand what she studied. Yet, she still wanted to learn more.

She would create a picture in her mind of what she thought was happening. Then she would ask if she was right.

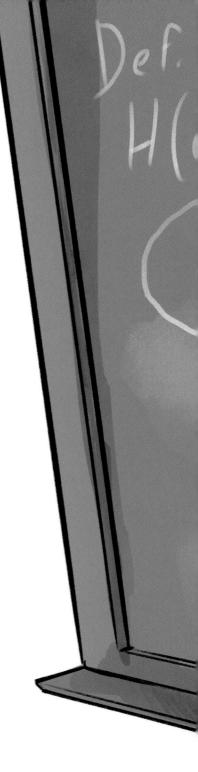

CHANGING MATH

Maryam got excited about studying the math behind curves. What is the shortest distance between two points? On a flat surface, it is a straight line. On a ball, it is a circle. What about a donut shape? What about a donut with many holes? No one knew these answers. That didn't stop Maryam.

She spent hours drawing her ideas. She spread huge pieces of paper on the floor. She sketched **diagrams** and **formulas**. Drawing her ideas helped her see problems in new ways. Maryam found the answer. She figured out how to find the shortest distance between two points on a donut shape.

Maryam's discovery helped mathematicians understand more about other areas of math. It gave old ideas new solutions.

Maryam continued to look for answers to math problems that had never been solved. She didn't mind if one problem took her years. She drew the pictures in her mind onto giant sheets of paper until she found an answer.

"It is like being lost in a jungle," she said. "And with some luck you might find a way out."

One day Maryam got an email. It said she won a big math prize. She thought it was a joke, but it was true! Maryam was the first woman and the first person from Iran to win the Fields Medal.

The Fields Medal
The Fields Medal is the highest honor in math. The medal is awarded every four years. Two to four people get it for doing great work. They are called the best mathematicians in the world.

Maryam liked challenges. "Life isn't supposed to be easy," she said. She found new answers to big questions. She also developed math tools. These tools help other people working on big questions.

The little girl from Iran grew up to do great things. Though Maryam died of breast cancer at the age of 40, her work lives on and continues to inspire other women and girls to find the exciting side of math.

TIME LINE

1977: Maryam is born in Tehrān, Iran on May 12.

1994 and 1995: Maryam wins gold medals at the International Mathematical Olympiad for high school students.

1999: Maryam earns a bachelor's degree in mathematics from Sharif University of Technology in Tehrān.

2004: Maryam earns a PhD from Harvard University in Massachusetts. Her PhD project is on geodesics, the math of curves.

2004: Maryam becomes an assistant professor of math at Princeton University in New Jersey.

2008: Maryam becomes a professor at Stanford University in California.

2008: Maryam marries Jan Vondrák.

2011: Maryam and Jan have a daughter, Anahita.

2013: Maryam is diagnosed with breast cancer.

2014: Maryam wins the Fields Medal.

2017: Maryam dies of breast cancer at age 40 on July 14.

GLOSSARY

ambition (am-BISH-uhn): a strong wish to reach a goal

competition (kahm-puh-TISH-uhn): a contest or game

diagrams (DYE-uh-GRAMS): drawings that show or explain something

disadvantage (dis-uhd-VAN-tij): less likely to succeed

formulas (FOR-myuh-luhs): groups of symbols that form a rule about how to do something

international (in-tur-NASH-uh-nuhl): something that involves two or more countries

mathematics (math-uh-MAT-iks): the study of numbers, shapes, quantities, and measurements and how they relate to one another

Persian (PUR-zhuhn): the language of the country of Iran, also called Farsi

INDEX

TEXT-DEPENDENT QUESTIONS

1. How did Maryam and Roya help each other?

2. How were high school girls in Iran at a disadvantage to the boys?

3. Why did Maryam like to draw her ideas?

4. How does Maryam think you can find the beauty in math?

5. What is the Fields Medal?

EXTENSION ACTIVITY

Can you show numbers without writing the numbers? What other math symbols do you know? Find out how other cultures write numbers. Look at how the ancient Romans, Egyptians, and Maya wrote numbers. What is helpful about each system?

ABOUT THE AUTHOR

M.M. Eboch also writes books as Chris Eboch. She likes to write about science and history. Her novel The Eyes of Pharaoh is a mystery in ancient Egypt. The Well of Sacrifice is an adventure about the Maya. She lives in New Mexico with her husband and their two ferrets.

ABOUT THE ILLUSTRATOR

Elena Bia was born in a little town in northern Italy, near the Alps. In her free time, she puts her heart into personal comics. She loves walking on the beach and walking through the woods. For her, flowers are the most beautiful form of life.

www.rourkeeducationalmedia.com

Quote sources: "A Tribute to Maryam Mirzakhani," AMS (The American Mathematical Society): http://www.ams.org/profession/mirzakhani; Erica Klarreich, "Meet the First Woman to Win Math's Most Prestigious Prize," Wired, (August 13, 2014): https://www.wired.com/2014/08/maryam-mirzakhani-fields-medal/; Kenneth Chang, "Maryam Mirzakhani, Only Woman to Win a Fields Medal, Dies at 40," The New York Times (July 16, 2017): https://www.nytimes.com/2017/07/16/us/maryam-mirzakhani-dead.html; "Maryam Mirzakhani," History of Mathematics Archive, MacTutor: https://mathshistory.st-andrews.ac.uk/Biographies/Mirzakhani/; Siobhan Roberts, "Maryam Mirzakhani's Pioneering Mathematical Legacy," The New Yorker, (July 17, 2017): https://www.newyorker.com/tech/annals-of-technology/maryam-mirzakhanis-pioneering-mathematical-legacy

Edited by: Hailey Scragg
Illustrated by: Elena Bia
Interior design by: Alison Tracey

Library of Congress PCN Data

Maryam Mirzakhani / M.M. Eboch
(Women in Science and Technology)
ISBN 978-1-73164-327-8 (hard cover)
ISBN 978-1-73164-291-2 (soft cover)
ISBN 978-1-73164-359-9 (e-Book)
ISBN 978-1-73164-391-9 (ePub)
Library of Congress Control Number: 2020945041

Rourke Educational Media
Printed in the United States of America
01-3502011937